Sacred Grids

Creating Crystal Grids with

Sacred Geometry

1

Sacred Grids

Creating Crystal Grids with Sacred Geometry

By

Sharon D. Anderson, Ph.D., R.M.T.

Dedication

This book is dedicated to Judy Hall whose work
with crystals is an inspiration to the world.
And
Plato, for his Platonic Solids that piqued my interest
in Sacred Geometry.

"We can easily forgive a child who is afraid of the dark; the real tragedy of life is when men are afraid of the light."

Plato

FORWARD

Sharon D. Anderson, Ph.D. has an amazing connection to all that is seen, and much of that which is unseen. She is at her very best in her newest book, Sacred Grids: Creating Grids with Sacred Geometry. This book is an excellent and very informative read. She finds an easy way to explain a complex subject. If you are curious about what Crystal Grids are and how to understand Sacred Geometry in creating, using, and maintaining these beautiful Crystal structures, I highly recommend using her book to guide you on your Grid journey. I truly believe in the power and use of Crystal Grids because they work! They help us find, and open magical spaces where hope, well-being, joy, harmony, love, healing, and so much more can thrive. Let Sharon show you how to use the healing light of Crystal Grids and Sacred Geometry and find these magical spaces. Once you get a taste of working with them, you will see them everywhere in nature and will want to fill your home with their incredible energy!!

Happy Gridding!
Kitty Elder, Gridologist

PREFACE

Amazing how things work and how the Divine Plan comes together.

Starting research on the sequel to *Creating Crystal Grids*, the information just dropped into my lap, literally.

The sequel was to cover creating grids using sacred geometric shapes for specific purposes. As the research progressed, more and more information surfaced. I have been studying this information for years but have not put it together until now. I used a reference to it in *Creating Crystal Grids* but this book, it appears, will be more in depth.

Occasionally, I refer to my Sacred Geometry Oracle Deck and felt that this time was most appropriate. The cards literally fell out of the deck in the order they were to be used.

<u>First Card</u>: World Grids – no surprise as I had already read excerpts from that book, *Anti-Gravity and World Grids* edited by David Hatcher Childress. It also stands for fellowship. The Sioux called the Earth the Creation Grid. Earth is also referred to as A Gaia Grid and my favorite, The Galactic Web.

<u>Second Card</u> – Pentagon – again, no big surprise but the pentagram stands for power and excellence. (Don't we have one of those in Washington D.C. already?) It also stands for regeneration and transcendence. When these points of the five sided pentagram are connected, it becomes the symbol of power and protection in the Wiccan tradition (a star).

<u>Third card</u>—Dodecahedron – again was no surprise because that is one of the Sacred Geometric Shapes to be covered in the book. It represents Divine Thought. It is the archetype of life and productiveness.

Thinking back to when I first became interested in Sacred Geometry, I couldn't even spell the names of the shapes.

I do hope that you will enjoy the process of this book. For me, the information is just flowing non-stop.

Eternal Hugs,

Sharon

Begun 9-09-2013

ACKNOWLEDGEMENTS:

I would be lost without Judy Hall's fabulous books on crystals: *The Crystal Bible, 101 Power Crystals, Crystal Prescriptions, and Crystal Healing.*

Plato's Platonic Solids and Sacred Geometry

Kitty Elder who kindled my interest in grids (she is a master in Gridology)

David Hatcher-Childress and his work: *Anti-Gravity and the World Grid.*

Becker-Hagens: *Pythagorean Cosmic Morphology*

Sacred Geometry Oracle Deck, by Francene Hart

Paul Jensen for his remarkable jewelry: *Tools for Evolution*, all created with Sacred Geometry.

Dwight Ritter for his extraordinary sense of graphics, help with the cover and inside illustrations.

Arthur Clark for his final editing making the copy ready for print.

For all of these sources,

I give grateful thanks...

Disclaimer

The information given here is not intended to be a substitute for treatment by a medical practitioner. Although crystals will work universally, further assistance should be sought from a suitably qualified Crystal healer.

SACRED GRIDS

CREATING CRYSTAL GRIDS WITH SACRED GEOMETRY

CONTENTS

CHAPTER ONE – SACRED GEOMETRY

The Language of Light

Sacred Geometry has often been referred to as "The Language of Light" or "Blueprint for All Creation" or "The harmonic configuration of the soul".

You will find Sacred Geometry in all of nature.

FIGURE 1 CENTER OF A SUNFLOWER

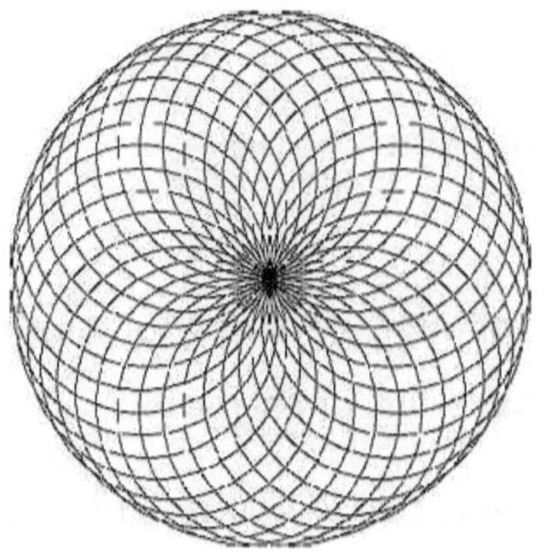

FIGURE 2 TORUS

FIGURE 3 A PERFECT TORUS IN THIS PINE CONE

FIGURE 4 INSIDE OF A BEEHIVE. PERFECT
ICOSAHEDRONS.

FIGURE 5 A PERFECT ICOSAHEDRON

FIGURE 6   SEE THE FLOWER OF LIFE IN THIS PERFECT
QUEEN ANN'S LACE?

FIGURE 7 THE FLOWER OF LIFE

The ancients believed that the experience of Sacred Geometry was essential to the education of the soul. They knew that these patterns and codes were symbolic of our own inner realm and the subtle structure of awareness. To them the "sacred" had particular significance involving consciousness and the profound mystery of awareness.

We begin with these shapes, as they are probably the oldest known. These are currently on display at the Ashmolean Museum in Oxford, England. They suggest a life of creative intelligence and exploration for the Neolithic craftsman who originally created them with animal skins and wrapped them using leather thongs.

"The experience of life in a finite, limited body is specifically for the purpose of discovering and manifesting supernatural existence within the finite."

Attributed to Pythagoras

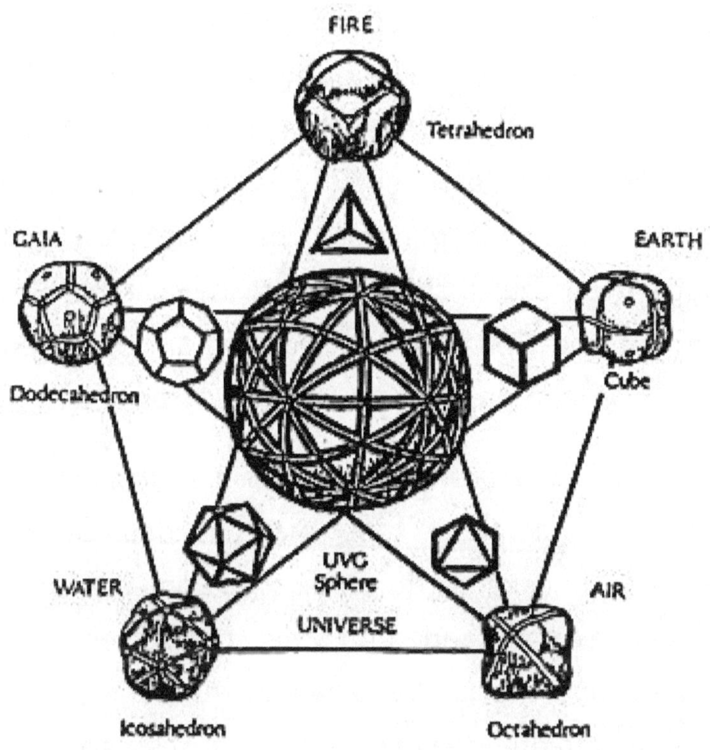

The Ancients studied Sacred Geometry. Socrates, Plato, Pythagoras, Archimedes, to name a few who have been instrumental in bringing it into consciousness. The most basic of these geometric shapes contains within them the entrance into the inner realms, which has inspired cultures and individuals since our inception here on Earth.

"Following from the teachings of Pythagoras, Plato applied mathematics to explain the structure of the Universe by using just three basic forms – the triangle, the square, and the pentagon. By using these three forms and the ratios that generate them, he was able to produce five regular solids, called the Platonic Solids, which are the Tetrahedron, Octahedron, Hexahedron (cube), Icosahedron, and the Dodecahedron (Pentagon).

"These five forms are the only possible forms in three-dimensional geometry that are bounded by plane surfaces having exactly the same shape and size. In each of these five forms, and in no other, the angles between the faces, and the angles between the edges, are the same size, and the area of each of the faces is the same."

Unknown Source

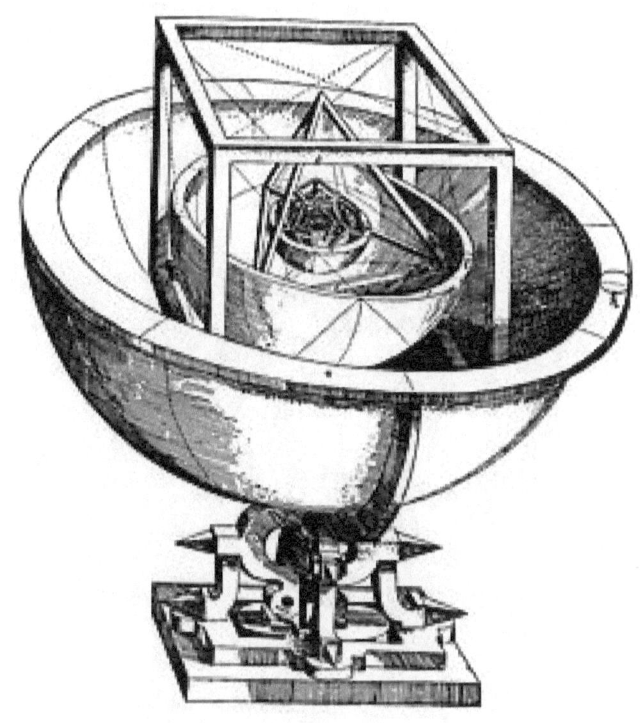

FIGURE 8: KEPLER'S PLATONIC SOLID MODEL OF THE SOLAR SYSTEM FROM MYSTERIUM COSMOGRAPHICUM (1596)

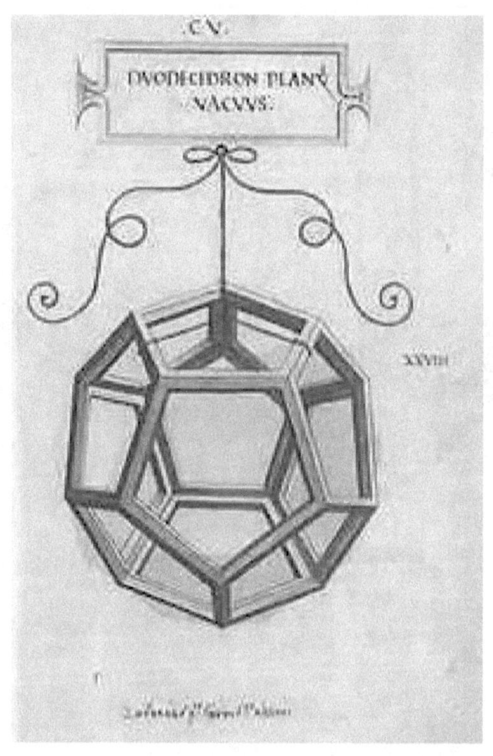

FIGURE 9 LEONARDO DAVINCI'S CONCEPT OF
THE DODECAHEDRON

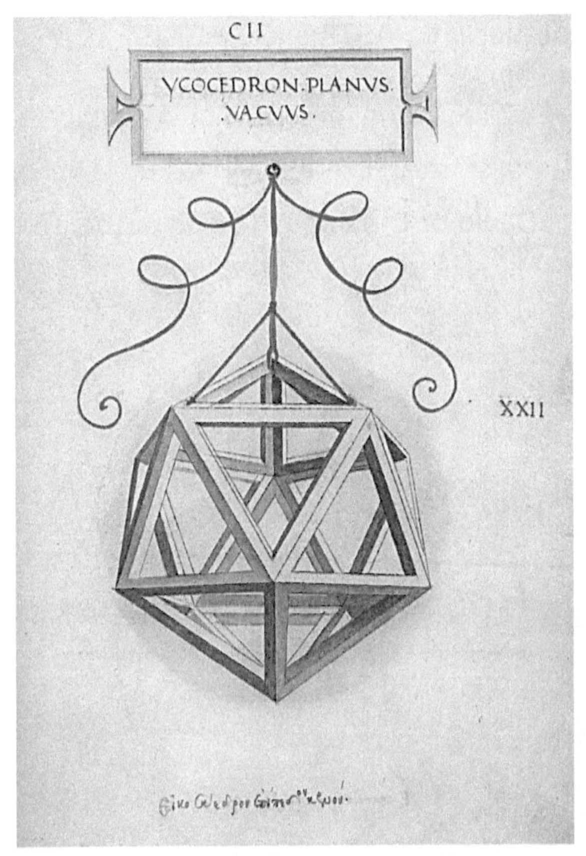

FIGURE 10 DAVINCI'S DRAWING OF THE ICOSAHEDRON

Here is another link, ASTROLOGY GRID

There are 12 sections of the Zodiac which is the 12 pointed stars or the FLOWER OF LIFE. The center has the Star of David or the two triangles of the Tetrahedron.

OUR LINKS TO SACRED GEOMETRY

Sacred Geometry is the link that ties us all together.

This link is often referred to as the

LANGUAGE OF LIGHT.

CRYSTALS are the DNA of the Earth

Note the cellular structure of a crystal.

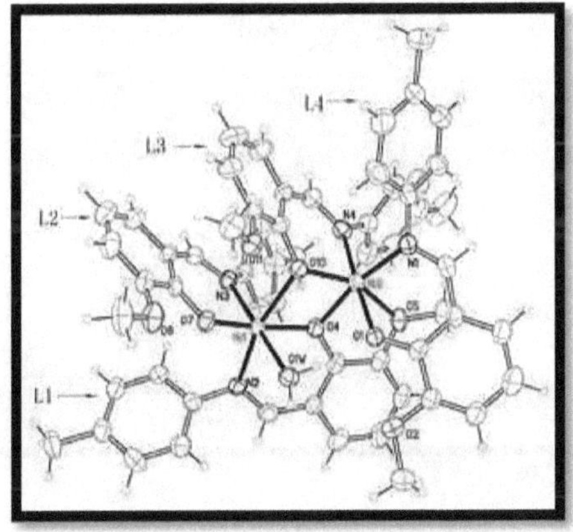

HUMAN DNA is the link to our Soul,

Our Consciousness

Can you see the similarities in this DNA Strand?

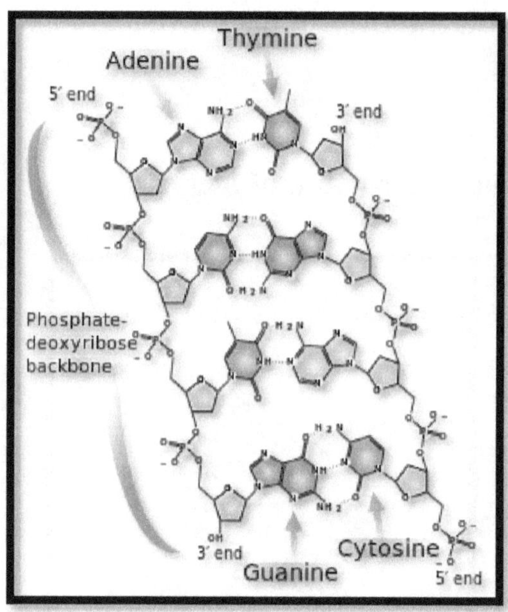

See the Dodecahedrons and Icosahedron?

Within this code are the human potential and the ability
to heal ourselves and the planet.

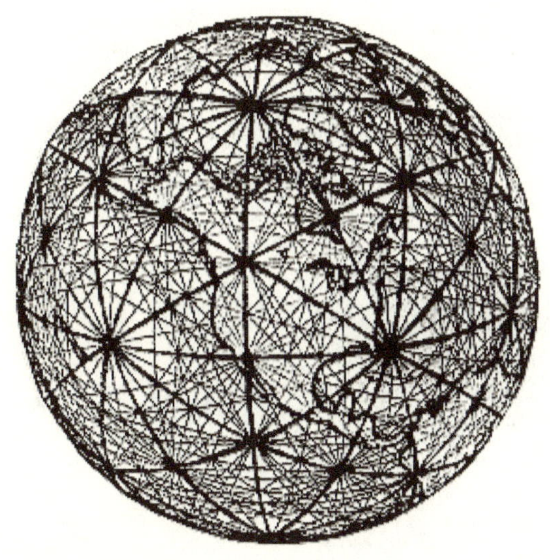

THE PLANETARY GRID SYSTEMS are the DNA of the Cosmos

The Earth has also been called the Gaia Grid and the Galactic Web. This includes ley lines, geomancy and the unified field theory. The Sioux called the Earth, the Creation Grid. Again, see the similarities?

Dodecahedrons and Icosahedrons.

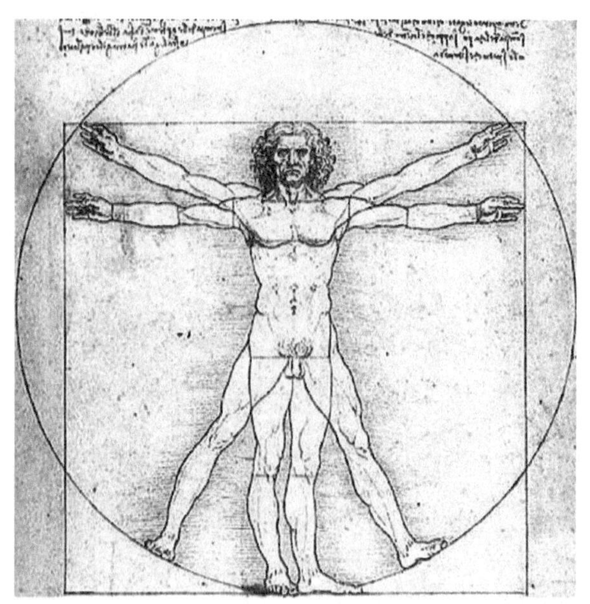

FIGURE 11 DAVINCI'S CONCEPT OF THE HUMAN BODY AND ITS RELATIONSHIP TO SACRED GEOMETRY

Da Vinci's drawing contains the entire system of Sacred Geometry including the Golden Portions of Phi. The mechanics of the human energy field , the Merkabah, can also be found in this drawing. The human body is in complete proportion to itself.

CHAPTER TWO – SACRED GEOMETRIC SHAPES

The five Platonic Solids are ideal, primal models of crystal patterns that occur throughout the world of minerals in countless variations. These are the only five regular polyhedral, the only five solids made from the same equilateral, equiangular polygons. Pure quartz crystal has been cut into these primal shapes for use in meditation, healing and manifestation.

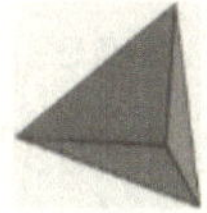

The Tetrahedron, or dimensional triangle. It has equal angles, edges of equal length , equal faces, and will fit within a sphere, represents Creation and Manifestation and Manifestation in Form. Within their structure they hold cosmic truths. It resonates with the Solar Plexus Chakra; the Color is Yellow, the Element is Fire. (4 faces)

The Hexahedron or (Cube) – represents *Grounding, Creation*- Grounding in Form. It has equal sides, equal angles, edges of equal length and six equal square faces. It represents solidity, strength and confined order. It holds earth and male energy. It resonates with the Base Chakra, Color is Red, and the Element is Earth.(six faces)

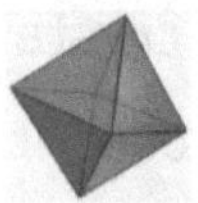

The Octahedron – represents the *Eight Paths to Enlightenment* in Integrative Form. It has equal sides, equal angles, edges of equal length and eight equal faces. It resonates with the Heart Chakra, the Color is Green, and the Element is Air. (Eight face)

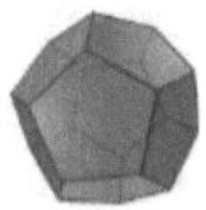

The Dodecahedron – Representing: the Twelve Faces of the Divine within, the Ascension and Mystery School, forms, the Spirit Chakras. It embodies divine thought or will and is the archetype of life and prosperity made visible. It is heaven, ether, prana and female. The Color is Gold, the Element is Ether. (12 faces)

The Icosahedron: represent Conscious Prayer and Transformation of Form. The Icosahedron has twenty equal triangular faces and represents the beginning of new consciousness. It resonates with the Navel Chakra, the Color is Blue, and the Element is Water. (20 faces)

CHAPTER THREE CRYSTALLINE GRID

The belief that our planet has a basic harmonic symmetry is very ancient. Socrates told his student Simmies, "My dear boy, the real earth viewed from above is supposed to look like one of those balls made out of twelve pieces of skin sewn together".

Three Russian scientists, after several years of research in Moscow, published their findings in *Khimiyai Zhizn* the popular science journal of the USSR Academy of Sciences entitled: "Is the Earth a Large Crystal?"

According to their hypothesis, the crystal can still be seen in twelve pentagonal slabs covering the surface of the globe – a Dodecahedron. As I view it, it more resembles an Icosahedron.

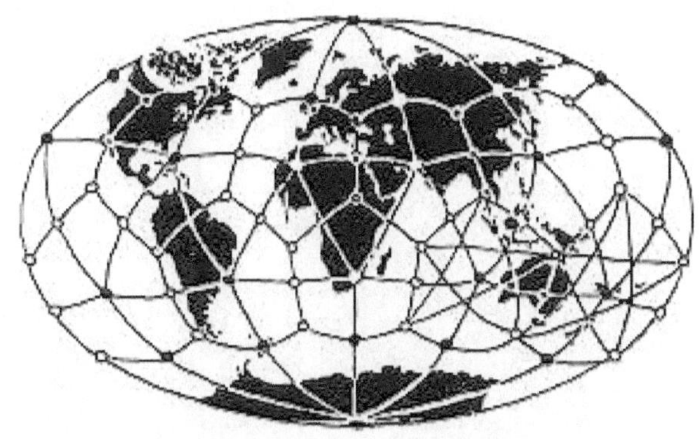

CHAPTER FOUR - THE WORLD GRID SYSTEM

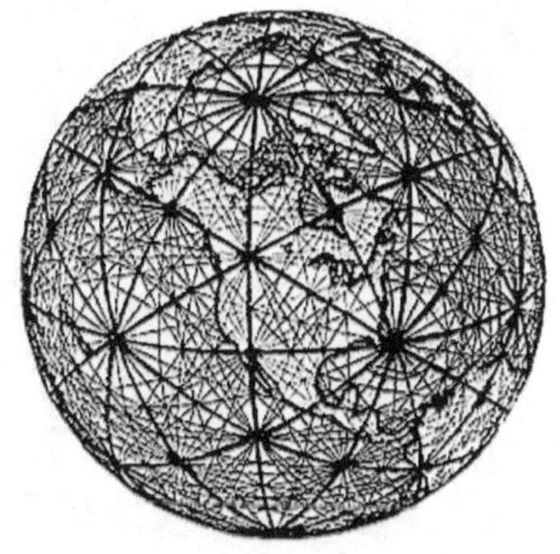

Becker and Hagens combine both the dodecahedron and the icosahedron when surrounding the planet with a grid system. Note the intersections or 'hot spots'. That is where most of the sacred sites have been established.

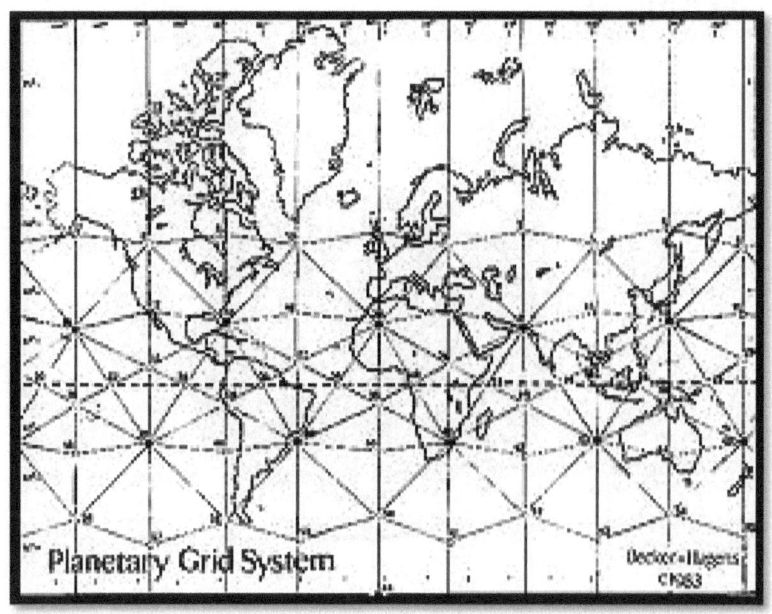

In this Planetary Grid system you can see the
Dodecahedron very clearly; note where they intersect.

Both of these illustrations come from *Anti-Gravity and
the World Grid* edited by David Hatcher Childress,
Unlimited Press, 1987.

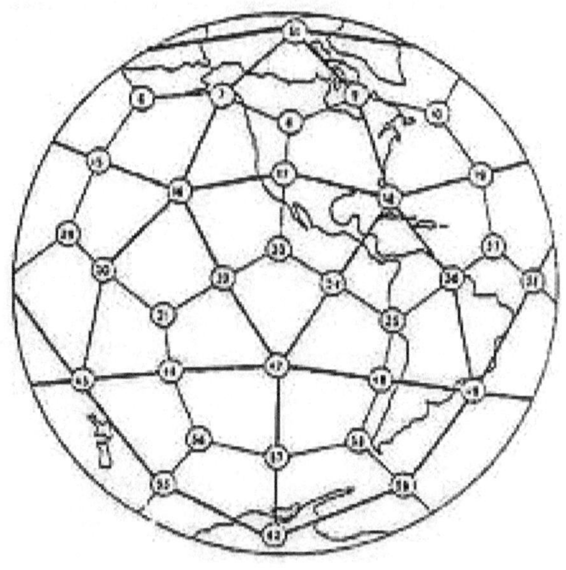

Megalithic Sites around the world plotted on the world grid from David Zink's book, *The Ancient Stones Speak* (Dutton, NYC, 1978)

Illustration from *Anti-Gravity and the World Grid*, David Hatcher Childress

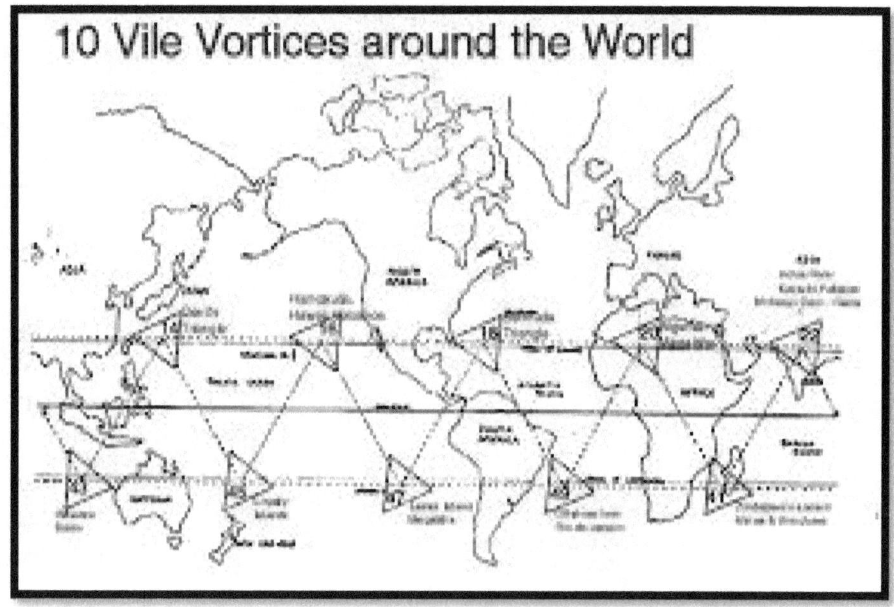

The ten vile vortices (originally taken from Ivan T. Sanderson's work). At these ten areas theoretically, magnet-gravitational anomalies take place. Nicholas R. Nelson, in his book, *Paradox*, believes that these vortex areas are entrances to other dimensions. Such 'doors' would account for strange disappearances and mysterious vanishings.

CHAPTER FIVE – THE GRID TEMPLATES

To create the templates for your sacred grids, we will use the five basic Platonic solids and a few more.

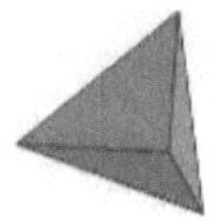 Tetrahedron

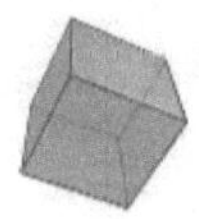 Hexahedron

 Octahedron

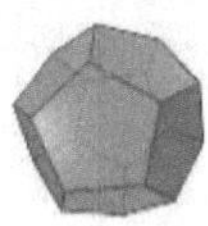 Dodecahedron

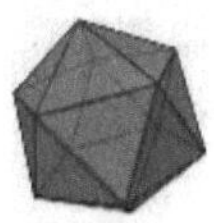 Icosahedron

CHAPTER SIX – BEFORE WE BEGIN

This information is taken from my previous book, *Creating Crystal Grids*. If you already have that book, thank you. I apologize for the repetition but there are a few additions.

If you have not read that first book, then here are the basic steps for creating your *Sacred Grids*.

What Are Grids And What Do We Use Them For?

Grids are energetic transmitters. They are like two-way radios that create an energetic field that will either bring energy down or send it out. When we create a grid, we are either calling in energy to be released into the environment for some purpose or intent or sending the energy out into the atmosphere for transmutation or for distant spiritual healing.

The most common configurations for grids are in geometric shapes, triangles, squares, stars, circles, etc.

When we create our grids we are calling upon the strength and the energetic qualities of these eternal geometric shapes to work in conjunction with these grids. We are asking for their assistance.

It is my belief that that the grids that we create work in

harmony with the sacred geometry shapes.

Grids have been used for centuries by all cultures.   They may not appear as the grids in this booklet but they are grids, never the less.

Stonehenge is a grid. A seven sided polygon or Heptagon

The pyramids are grids, the Octahedron

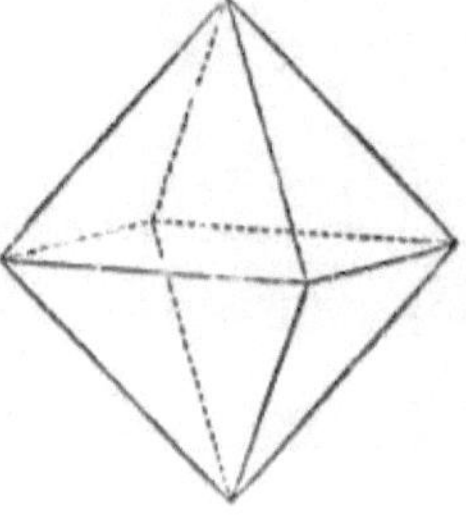

CREATING CRYSTAL GRIDS

The grids shown in this book are composed of several crystals or stones in a certain alignment. You get to choose which alignment you want to use as you plan your grid. In all of the grids, we use both polished or raw stones, and natural or created points

A WORD ABOUT CRYSTAL ENERGY:

Each crystal carries a <u>definite energy</u>; soothing, calming, energetic, etc....

Each crystal has <u>specific properties</u>; protection, attraction, grounding, etc....

Each crystal has definite <u>healing or metaphysical qualities</u> for specific die-eases, body parts or organs.

Most crystal books will give you all of that information. If you carry a crystal on your person, know what energies it emanates so that you will get all of the benefits of that particular stone.

If you decide the purpose or intent for your grid is to send a dear one healing for a specific condition, for example cancer, you would choose one or two of the following stones: Amethyst, Carnelian, Magnetite (Lodestone) with Smokey Quartz, Melanite Garnet, Petalite, Red Jasper, Smokey Quartz, or Sugilite. (All stones listed here came from *Crystal Prescriptions* by Judy Hall)

Working together in harmonic placement, the proposed grid will send out an energetic field that will accomplish whatever intent you as the originator of the grid, asks.

Choose wisely, set the grid, and you will create a force that will allow these energies to permeate the atmosphere and bring your intent to fruition

CAUTION: crystals and grids are only to be used for the HIGHEST GOOD FOR ALL.

RECOMMENDED REFERENCES: *The Crystal Bible, The Crystal Bible 2 and Crystal Prescriptions,* by Author Judy Hall are our recommendation to begin with or any book on crystals you prefer.

CHAPTER SEVEN – INTENT FOR THE GRID

<u>YOUR REASON OR INTENT FOR CREATING THE GRID IS YOUR FIRST STEP</u>.

Protection for your home, or your person,

Harmony and balance in the workplace,

Amping up your level of creativity,

Energize vitamins, elixirs, remedies,

Healing someone at a distance or yourself

For use in Meditation

Creating sacred space,

Healing of the Earth after disaster or mis-use,

Cleansing, purifying or amplifying space, food or anything,

Bringing more harmonious relationships into your life,

Next,

SELECTING YOUR CRYSTALS:

Now that you have your intent in mind, begin to select the appropriate crystals, keeping in mind what you wish to accomplish.

The mineral kingdom (crystals and stones mostly) resonate well with the numbers 3, 4, and 6 or multiples' of those numbers.

Do you want to send healing energy to a dear friend who is far away and undergoing chemotherapy? Choose Smokey Quartz and Clear Quartz. You could also send them a Smokey Quartz to keep on their person to alleviate some of the stress of the treatment.

Do you wish to attract a 'special someone' into your life or to enhance the relationship already in progress? Set up a grid with Rose Quartz, the Love Crystal. Or place a chunk of Rose Quartz in the Relationship corner (far right) of your bedroom.

FIGURE 12 ROSE QUARTZ TUMBLED

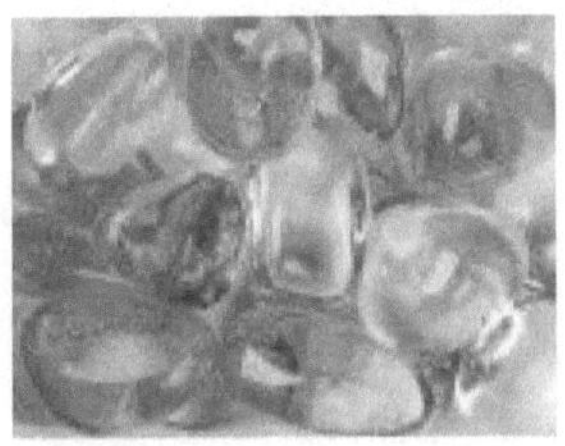

FIGURE 13 SMOKEY QUARTZ TUMBLED

FIGURE 14 CLEAR QUARTZ TUMBLED

Do you need more wealth, prosperity and abundance in your life? (Who doesn't) then create a grid using Citrine or Tree Agate or Jade, any or all of these crystals are great at drawing in wealth, abundance, and prosperity. Remember to place some of them in the farthest left rear corner from the front door of your home (The Wealth corner of your house or apartment).

FIGURE 15. CITRINE CLUSTER

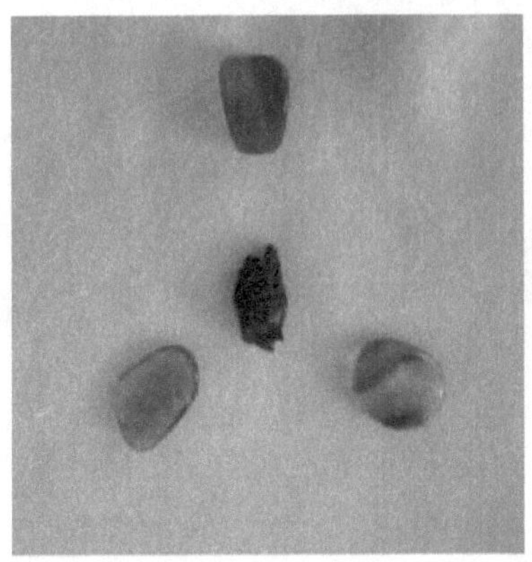

THREE STONE GRIDS 1 MASCULINE

A THREE (3) stones grid, figure 1, is used to manifest.

Sending energy up or out

This grid has three Fluorite crystals and the center is a Tektite.

Intent: Psychic protection and healing.

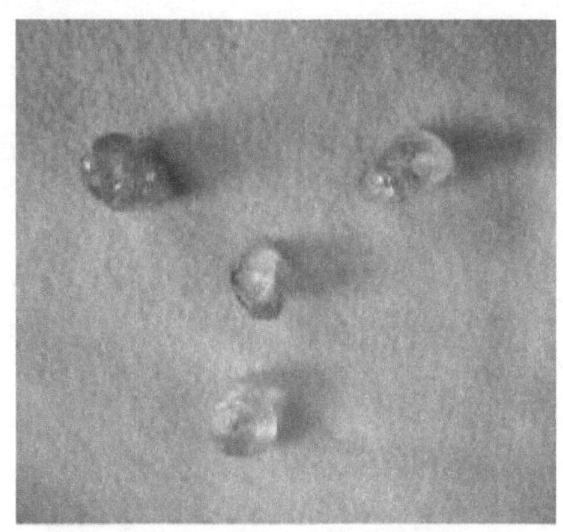

THREE STONE GRIDS 2 FEMININE

This configuration is used to bring the energy down

This grid has three tumbled Citrine with a Clear Quartz center.

Intent: Manifesting prosperity and abundance

A FOUR (4) stone grid is usually used for bringing balance and alignment into a situation or group.

Also to bring in the Four Directions

It has two Labradorite, two Clear Quartz with an Iron Pyrite center stone

Intent: Clearing out old energies and replacing them with newer, more powerful ones.

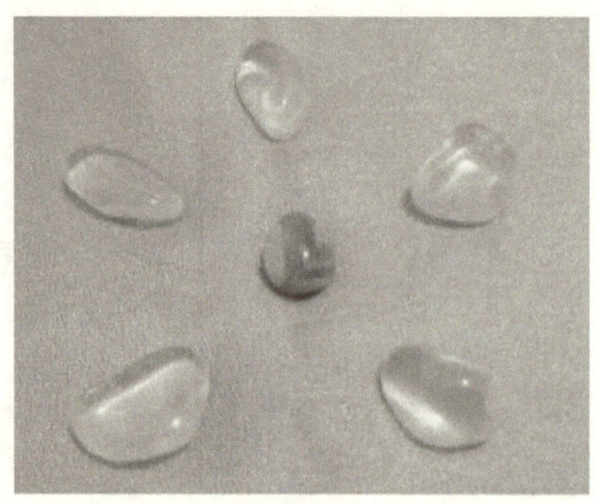

FIVE STONE GRIDS 1 PENTAGRAM OR THE DODECAHEDRON

A FIVE (5) stone grid forms a star, or a pentagram.

This grid is composed of five Clear Quartz crystals with a Citrine center.

Intent: High energy distance healing.

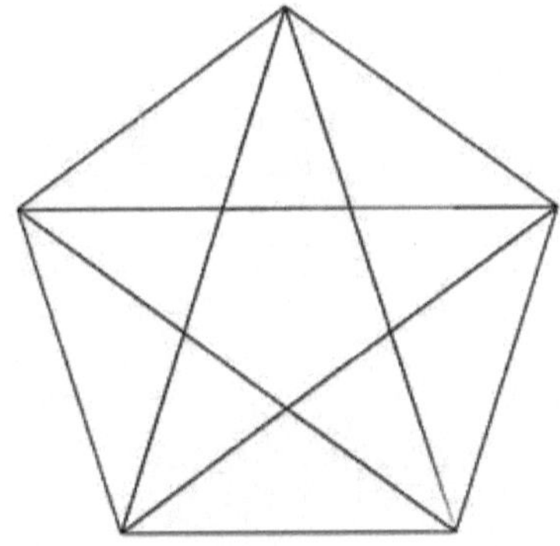

If directed to a person or situation, the name and location can be written on a piece of paper and placed under the center stone, or a photograph of the person.

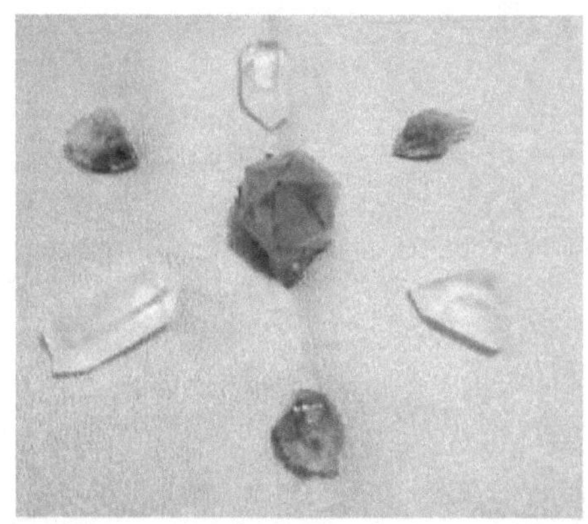

SIX STONE GRIDS - STAR OF DAVID OR THE HEXAGON

A SIX (6) stone grid, usually the one most commonly used, will generate a pretty forceful focus of energy. This is the six pointed Star of David or the Merkabah. You can see the triangles created by the clear crystal points pointing up and the three Amethyst points creating the triangle facing down. There is an Amethyst perfect point in the center to generate out the healing qualities of the Amethyst.

Intent: sending healing energy to overcome addictions.

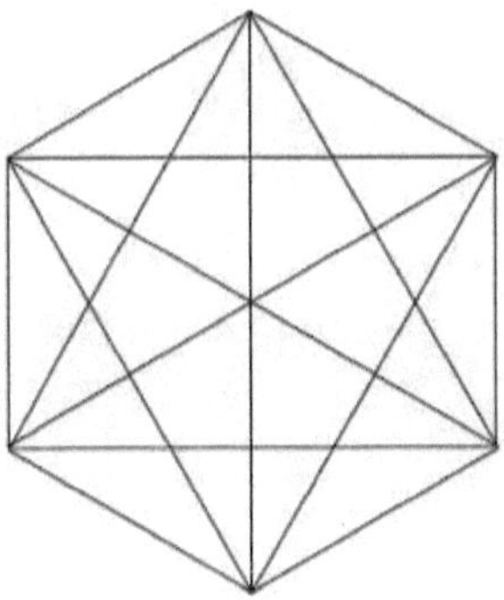

EIGHT STONE GRIDS 1 THE OCTAGON OR THE BAGUA

THE EIGHT STONE GRID (8) is a double of the four and also a very commonly used figuration:

This one was created for clearing smog.

It has four (4) Amethyst Points and four (4) Clear Quartz points with an Amethyst Point in the center.

Intent: Clearing geopathic stress and smog from a room

Below is the Bagua from Feng Shui common in the Chinese culture

Feng Shui works with nature to create perfect balance and harmony everywhere.

It has 8 sides…

TWELVE STONE GRID IS THE FLOWER OF LIFE

THE TWELVE STONE GRID (12) carries a great amount of energy, should be placed cautiously, and with a very high intent. Use this grid for bringing in peace and harmony in a world situation, or to help balance the environment.

This particular grid was created to spread harmony within a new corporation. It is composed of six Amazonite, for clearing and protection, and six Labradorite, to bring in the higher vibrations of consciousness. Another words, we wanted the officers to think "out of the box".

The Flower of Life symbol has been found in the pyramids and in many ancient temples and buildings around the world. It contains EVERY SACRED GEOMETRY SHAPE.

CHAPTER EIGHT - THE TETRAHEDRON

The Tetrahedron is one of the five three dimensional geometric shapes known as the Platonic Solids, or the Pythagorean Cosmic Morphology. Each shape has equal angles, edges of equal length, and equal faces. This shape will fit within a sphere. Each shape can be found in the FLOWER OF LIFE. Within their structure, they hold cosmic wisdom and information.

The Tetrahedron or dimensional triangle represents Creation and Manifestation and Manifestation in Form. It resonates with the Solar Plexus Chakra; the Color is Yellow, the Element is Fire. (4 faces)

Use this shape to send energy up and out.

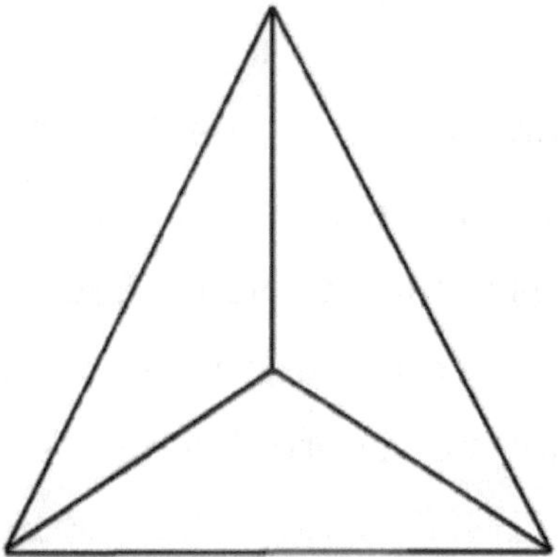

The Tetrahedron is the simplest of these shapes with four equal triangular faces. It also represents the male side and is the place of ACTION. This is the fire of ambition and understanding that will be needed to activate ideas or to complete projects already in process. Use this shape to bring ideas and projects into fruition. It also represents the Trinity, the Connection with the Divine.

Use this shape to bring the energy down.

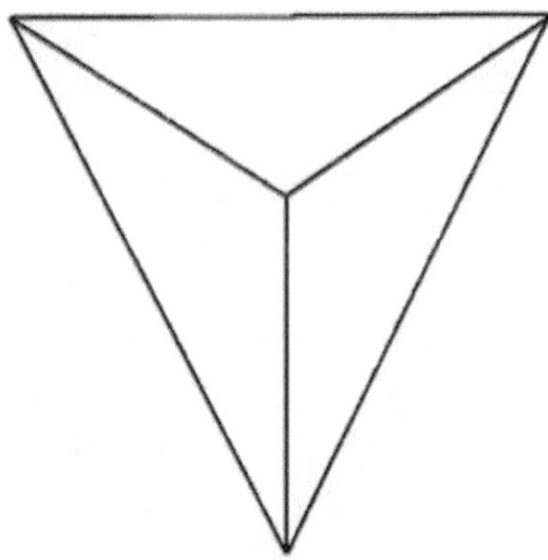

Here are two grids for this configuration.

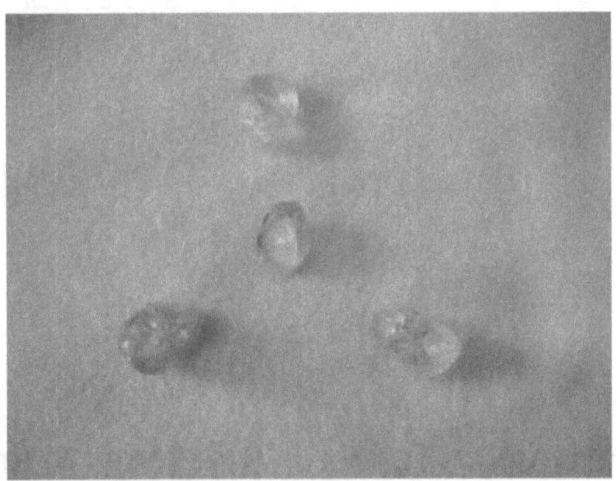

We used three Citrine with Clear Quartz in the center. As it is an ascending triangle, male configuration. Use it to send out prosperity and abundance to anyone you would like. You can write the name and location on a folded piece of paper and place it under the center stone.

Three Fluorite with a Tektite in the center to amplify. This is the descending triangle, the female configuration. Use this one to bring in protective energy to anyone you prefer by placing their name and location on a folded slip of paper under the center stone.

These configurations can be used for any number of purposes.

This jewelry from "Tools for Evolution" was created by Paul Jensen from the Jewelry Factory. The jewelry is created for integrating this energy into daily life. The shape, The Angelic Star Cut is the inverted tetrahedron - the feminine side. This stone is Amethyst. The jewelry pieces featured in this book can be purchased at http://www.exquisitecrystals.com

The second Stone is the Star of David cut in Rose quartz. It is the male cut of the triangle. This cut has the female cut on the other side of the stone creating the Star of David bringing protection, harmony and balance to the person wearing the stone.

CHAPTER NINE - THE HEXAHEDRON

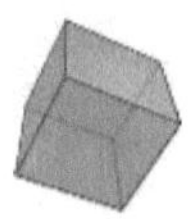

The Hexahedron or (Cube) – represents *Grounding, Creation*- Grounding in Form. It resonates with the Base Chakra, Color is Red, and the Element is Earth.

The cube has six equal square faces. It represents solidity, strength and confined order. It holds earth and male energy.

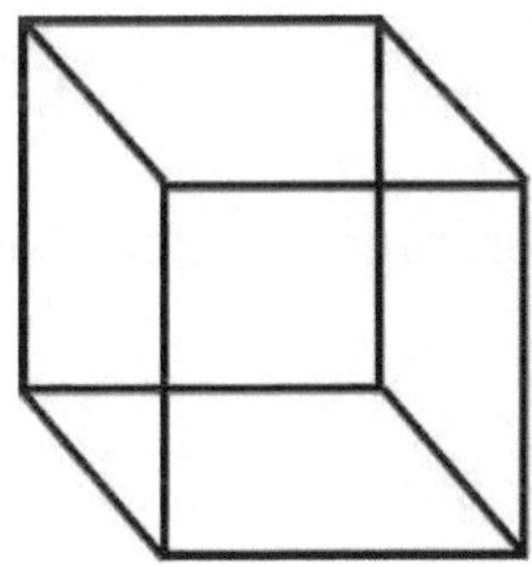

Use this solid connection to bring ideas from the imaginary into the realm of substance and manifest things.

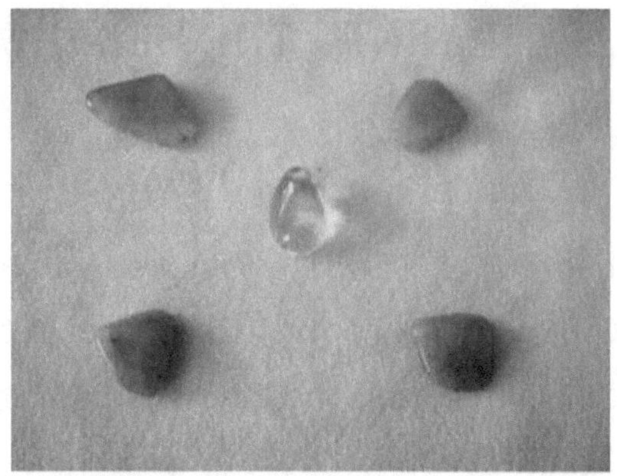

For this grid we used 4 Green Aventurine and clear quartz for the center.

Using the Green Aventurine has several purposes:

1. Protects and resonates w/heart chakra for healing.

2. Neutralizes environmental pollution from computers and cell phones.

3. Positive stone for prosperity and attracting abundance.

Whatever you choose, the cube will assist. Note: the center stone in these flat grids create the depth of the shape. On this grid, the clear quartz creates the actual cube.

This second grid has 2 Labradorite and 2 Clear Quartz, with an Iron Pyrite for the center stone.

Labradorite is highly mystical and protective, a bringer of Light,

It raises consciousness and connects with universal energies.

Deflects unwanted energies from the aura, prevents energy leakage.

It aligns the physical and etheric bodies, accesses spiritual purpose.

Pyrite augments intelligence, mental stability, logic, and analysis, creativity, channeling abilities, memory, optimism, practicality and willpower.

Sacred Geometry Jewelry: This pendant is an EARTH STAR or Hexahedron in Siberian Blue Quartz..

The Octahedron – represents the *Eight Paths to Enlightenment* in Integrative Form. It resonates with the Heart Chakra, the Color is Green, and the Element is Air. (8 faces)

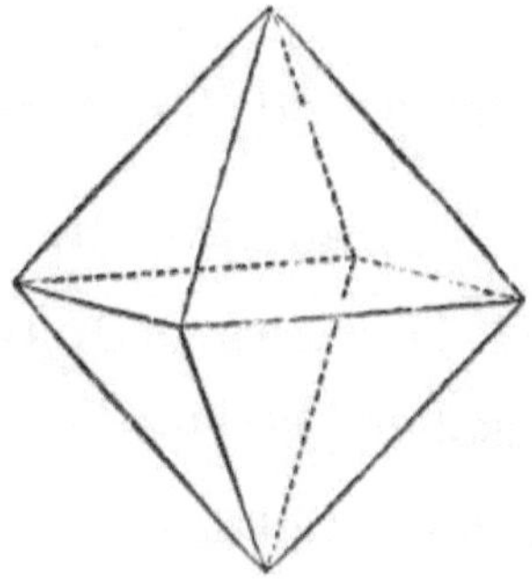

I call this the Ascension Grid. (7 stones)

Composed of 2 Labradorite to bring in Higher Consciousness and Connects with Universal Energies, Two Fluorite for dissolving blocks and bring in protection, Two Clear Quartz for amplification and Pyrite for the center to Augment Intelligence and Mental Stability.

This grid was created to dedicate a new Spiritual Center.

Sacred Geometry Jewelry.

This is the Ascension Pendant, clear quartz with a Starburst Citrine. You can see the Tetrahedron in the cut of the clear quartz.

CHAPTER ELEVEN – THE DODECAHEDRON

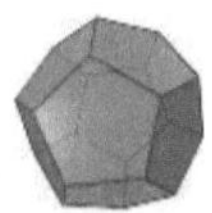

The Dodecahedron – Representing: the Twelve Faces of the Divine within, the Ascension and Mystery School, forms, the Spirit Chakras. The Color is Gold, the Element is Ether. (12 faces)

I view the Dodecahedron as a pentagon or the Star within 10 points.

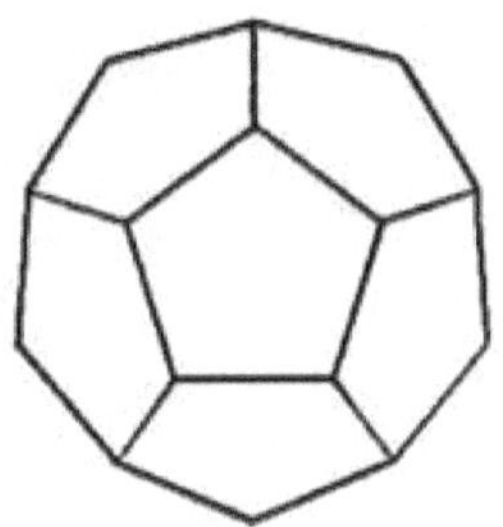

This grid would use 5 crystals set as a star pattern and 10 crystals surrounding it.

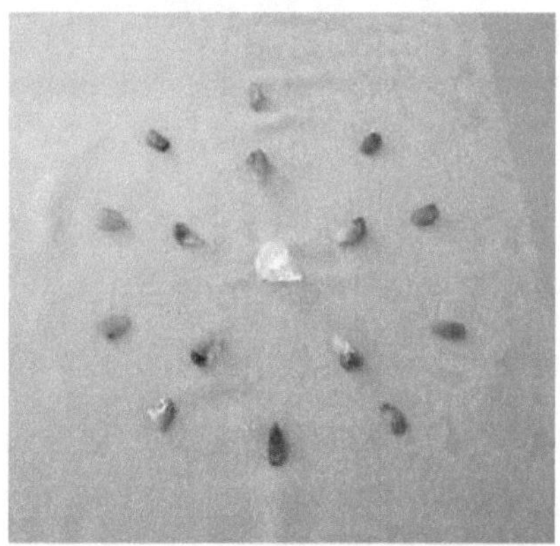

We have used 5 Amethyst points for center ring and 10 Chrysoprase for the outside. The center is a Russian Lemurian Ice quartz. The purpose is to send harmony and balance to a hostile situation.

SACRED GEOMETRY JEWELRY:

Paul Jensen of the Jewelry Factory in Wyoming designed the jewelry you see in this book. The cut in these pendants is a Pentagram, the dodecahedron. It also resembles the hive of a bee

THE PENTAGRAM

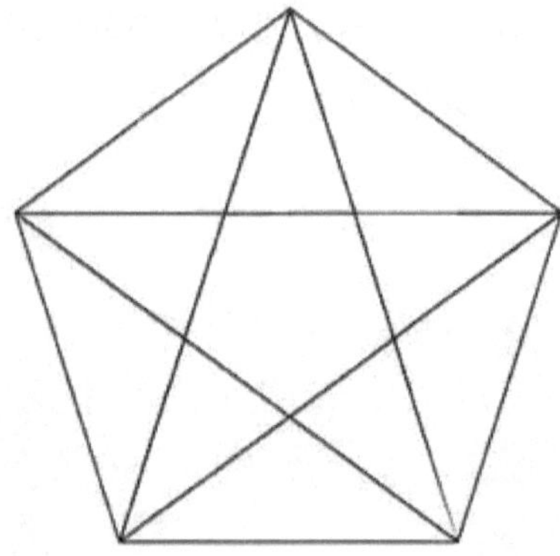

A five sided geometric figure, a Dodecahedron, holds energy that represents power, excellence, regeneration and transcendence. When the mid-points of each side of the pentagon are connected, they form a star. This shape is called a Pentagram. Is a symbol of power and protection in the Wiccan tradition.

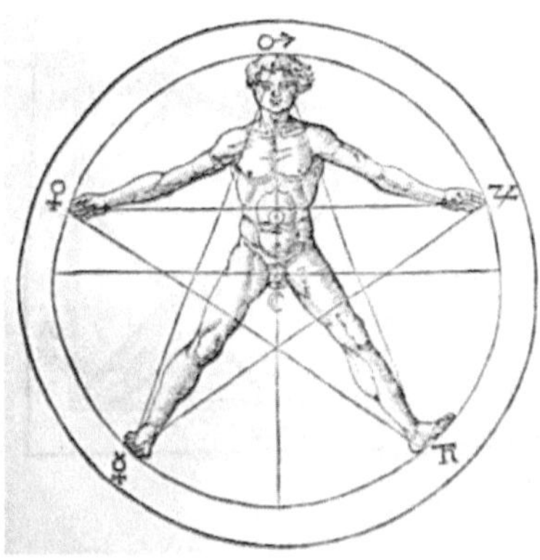

Man measured in a Pentagram… all in concise proportion. The center of the human body is just below the navel on the pubic bone.

CHAPTER TWELVE - THE ICOSAHEDRON

The Icosahedron: represent Conscious Praye*r* and Transformation of Form. It resonates with the Navel Chakra, the Color is Blue, and the Element is Water. (20 faces)

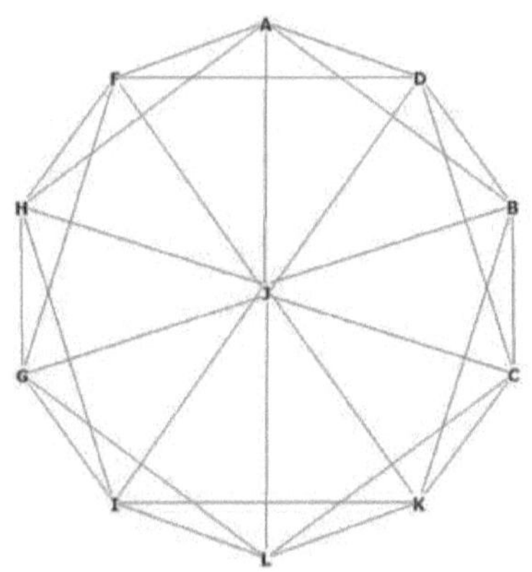

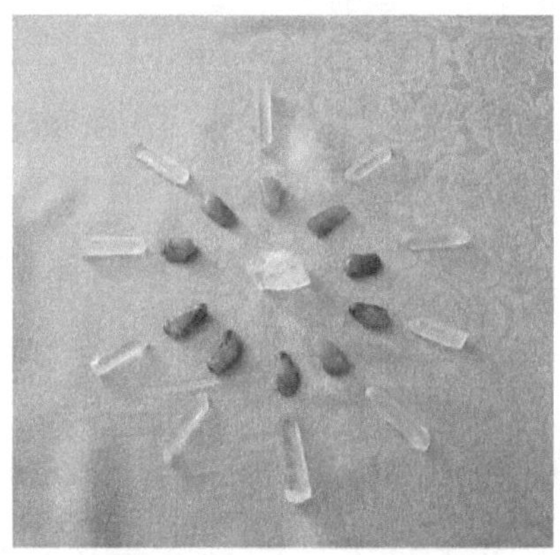

This grid has a double whammy... I used 10 Chrysoprase surrounded with 10 Laser Points focusing extremely strong energy into the center stone of Russian Lemurian Ice Quartz.

Intent: to bring peace and harmony to world conflicts.

THE FLOWER OF LIFE

The Language of Silence, the Language of Light.
The Blueprint of all Creation.

"This pattern, called the Flower of Life is one of the most universal pieces of sacred geometry available to us. This figure was found burned into the granite on the walls of an old Egyptian temple, the Temple of Osiris, in Abydos, Egypt. This same symbol has also been found in more than 18 countries around the globe from Turkey to Tibet from China to the Yucatán. The Flower of Life has imprinted its wisdom upon humankind for centuries. It represents a lattice of pure life force, containing all of our cellular memory, and it becomes the matrix of all matter.

"The flower of life is an Akashic information system, meaning it contains records of all that was, all that is, and all that will be. The messages it offers are both intimately personal and universal. It is made of 19 concentric circles or 19 interlocking spheres."

Information taken in part from Francene Hart's *Sacred Geometry Oracle Deck.*, Bear and Company, Rochester, VT.©2001 by Francene Hart,

Every Sacred Geometry shape can be found within this pattern.

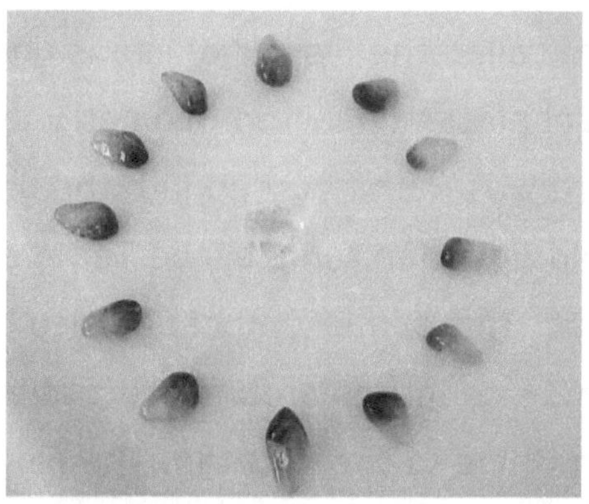

A 12 stone grid, the Flower of Life.

We used 12 Amethyst points with a crystal Icosahedron in the center. Intent: Raising world consciousness.

This is the Flower of Life pendant created by Paul Jensen as one of his Tools for Evolution series. This stone is the Russian Lemurian Ice quartz. It creates the 12 pointed star associated with Christ Consciousness and the restoration of Divine Order. I wear my pendant almost every day.

Flower of Life Crop Circle, Photo by Lucy Pringle

If you look carefully, you will see the drawing found in
the Temple of Osiris in Abydos, Egypt. This etching into
the wall of the temple is believed to be over
10,500 BCE

OTHER GEOMETRY SHAPES

VESICA PISCIS

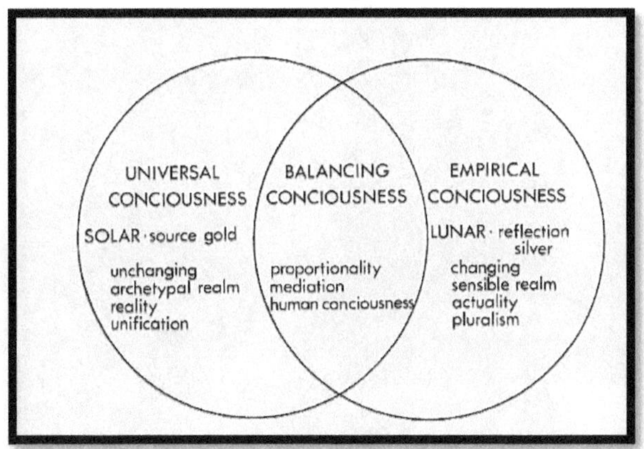

One of the ways to view the Vesica Piscis is as a representation of the intermediate realm which shares both the unchanging and changing principals of the eternal and the transitory.

Human consciousness thus functions as the mediator, balancing the two complementary poles of consciousness. The Vesica Piscis has often been referred to as the birth portal. It is the end center penetration of two circles or spheres representing two holes. It becomes a birth portal where they intersect. It is the birthing place where people and ideas are joined in mutual understanding and common ground.

For this grid, we used two 8 stone circles overlapping as does its sacred geometry origin. This figure is found within the Flower of Life and is thought to also be the symbol of two coming together creating the one.
This grid is created using 8 Chrysoprase and 8 Citrine.

Intent: to bring balance into a newly formed business. The Citrine was chosen for abundance and prosperity and the Chrysoprase to encourage fidelity in business.

THE KABALAH

From Mystical Judaism, the Kabalah diagrams The Tree Of Life and holds instructions for self-actualization and growth. It is the power within. The Kabalah offers guidelines for conscious self exploration. It contains 10 archetypes to be used for self growth. The geometry of the Tree of Life is also encoded within the figure called the Flower of Life. It is often referred to as the Tree of Knowledge, The Tree of Perfection, or the World Tree. In the Mayan tradition it is the 'Raised Up Sky Tree'.

In the figure above, the Kabalah is derived from The Flower Of Life. To set a grid, we would need 10 stones.

We used 5 Green Aventurine and 5 Fluorite

Green Aventurine is a heart healer bringing all conditions back into balance and Fluorite draws off negative energies and stress of all kinds. It reorganizes anything within the body that is not in perfect order.

Intent: Self-actualization and growth.

THE CIRCLE

FIGURE 16 DUOMO LUCCA CATHEDRALE, LACQUES LABYRINTHE

Wall Maze in Lucca Cathedral, Italy, (Probably Medieval)

A simple circle grid: We used 8 Fluorite with a Raw Rose Quartz in the center.

Intent: Brings stability to groups, linking them to a common cause. The Raw Rose Quartz in the center manifests Unconditional Love.

METATRON'S CUBE

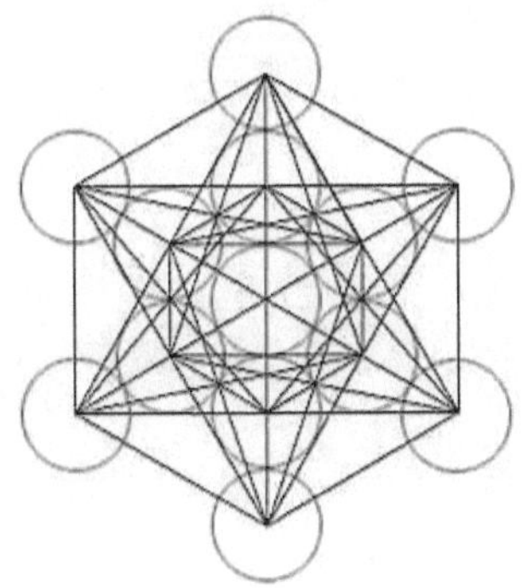

Metatron's Cube is a metaphor for all problems solving, not only in third-dimensional reality but in other dimensions as well. It also represents relationships with/within the community, either local or global.

Within the geometry of this shape, all five of the Platonic Solids reside. There is the joining of the male and female energies (the two triangles or Tetrahedrons, one pointing up, the other pointing down) by joining those energies, something new is created, and balance is manifested.

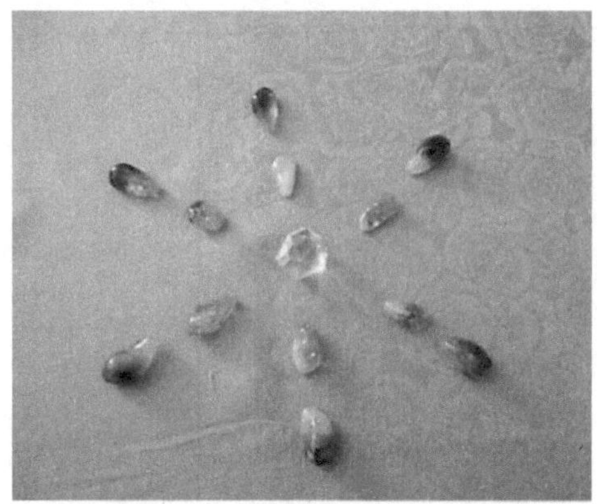

This very powerful grid is comprised of 6 Citrine (center) points and 6 Amethyst Points (outer radius) with a clear crystal Icosahedron in the center.

Intent: A new Yoga Center wanted to manifest the abundance and prosperity of the Citrine but didn't want to lose the connection with the Higher Spiritual Energies.

HEPTAGON

The Heptagon is a seven sided polygon of reverence. It represents movement through cycles. Seven days a week, seven chakras, seven rays of a rainbow, seven seas, and seven planets (although we do have many more) seven musical notes, seven stages of transformation. . . Stonehenge is based on the number seven.

It also represents the harmony in the cycles of life.

This seven sided Heptagon has 7 Amazonite with a Raw Rose Quartz in the center.

We chose Amazonite for soothing emotional trauma and the Rose Quartz to manifest Universal Love.

This is an overview of the Mysticism of Stonehenge. A diagram of Stonehenge is in the center.

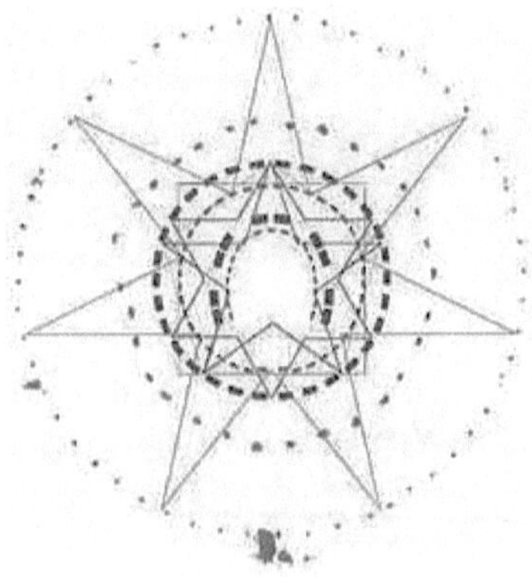

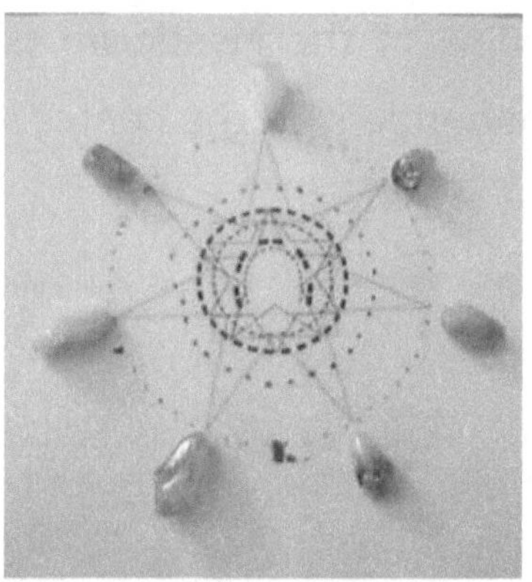

Here we used 7 Citrine Points for balance and harmony.
Citrine balances the Yin and Yang.

SACRED GRIDS FOR CHAKRA ALIGNMENT

DIMENSIONAL CHAKRA GRIDS

Here is a suggested list of the Chakra Hierarchy Grids Dimensions refer to levels of consciousness and are not actual living spaces. Each dimension is a level of conscious understanding or enlightenment.

Third dimensional chakra grid - Chakras one through seven. (7)

Fourth dimensional chakra grid - Chakras eight through eleven.(4)

Fifth dimensional chakra grid - Chakras twelve through eighteen.(7)

Sixth dimensional chakra grid – Chakras nineteen to twenty two.(4)

Seventh dimensional chakra grid - Chakras twenty-three through twenty-nine.(7)

Eighth dimensional chakra grid - Chakras thirty to thirty-three.(4)

Ninth dimensional chakra grid - Chakras thirty-four to forty.(7)

Tenth dimensional Chakra grid – Chakras forty-one to forty-four. (4)

The 7 and 4 sequence..

COLOR

Let's talk about color first.

Beginning with the three primary colors:

Blue represents our will to be, our will to live, our physical being.

Red symbolizes love, compassion, devotion, emotional being.

Yellow embodies spirit, creative intelligence, our intellectual being.

Clear or no color gives us all seven colors.

Black is the absence of all color.

Red, orange, and yellow are our warm colors

Green is neutral

Blue, indigo and violet are cool colors.

If you wish to assist someone with a chronic illness, or lack of energy, use warm colors.

If there is an acute illness, that signifies too much energy so a cool color is needed.

Any illness requiring balance – use green or a neutral.

Using a color wheel, we can look at the basic color, its opposite color and the color to bring in balance.

CHAKRA	COLOR	OPPOSITE	BALANCE
Earth	Brown	Black	White/clear
Root	Red	Green	White/violet
Sacral	Orange	Blue	Purple/indigo
Solar plexus	Yellow	Purple	Blue
Heart	Green	Red	Pink
Etheric heart	Aqua	White	Green/blue
Throat	Blue	Orange	Yellow
Third eye	Indigo/purple	Yellow	Orange
Crown	White/violet	Black/turquoise	red

To incorporate this into your grids, the outer stones could be the color for the Chakra and the center stone its opposite or the balance one.

Another suggestion is using a grid with stones, 2 of each or 3 of each, depending on the shape of the grid with the balance stone in the center.

Our Chakras vibrate to all of those colors previously mentioned.
Each Chakra is connected to a specific area of our lives. If there are imbalances or blockages in a Chakra, that can create specific areas of dis-ease. This can be healed by placing an appropriate color crystal onto the chakra.

If that is not possible, then create a grid using crystals in that color which will resonate to the Chakra and cause a subtle healing. You can direct the energy to a specific person or location by writing that person's name and/or location on a slip of paper and placing it under the center stone.

SACRED GRIDS FOR CHAKRA HEALING

For this section of the book, using sacred grids to create chakra healing, we will incorporate Judy Hall's 12 chakra system plus a few more that I have inserted instead of the seven basic systems which is already included.

The information for the crystals that were used was derived from Judy Hall's *Crystal Bible*.

1. HIGHER EARTH CHAKRA

This grid uses 8 Bloodstone with a center stone of Red Jasper.

Intent: Bloodstone is used for cleansing and stabilizing.

Bloodstone-is a dark green chalcedony with red flecks. Brings abundance, rain, alignment, generosity, smooth energy flow, idealism, good fortune, organizational abilities and purification.

It purifies the blood and detoxifies liver, intestines, kidneys, spleen and bladder. Regulates and supports blood flow, aids circulation. Position as appropriate, wear continually for good health. Tape over thymus as an immune stimulator. Place in bowl of water beside bed for peaceful sleep.

2. EARTH CHAKRA – BETWEEN THE FEET

We used 4 Smokey quartz in a Hexahedron or cube for grounding and protecting.

Smokey Quartz - Brazil - effective for ailments of the abdomen, hips and legs. Relieves pain, headaches, dissolves cramps, strengthens the back, fortifies the nerves and aids assimilation of minerals. Regulates liquids within the body. Position at base chakra, under pillow or as pendant.

Smokey quartz is naturally a balanced stone containing the necessary brown tint but also having the white/clear balancing color.

Imbalances in this Chakra can lead to physical discomfort and feelings of helplessness. Imbalances may also attract geopathic stress and toxic pollutants.

3. THE ROOT CHAKRA AT THE BASE OF SPINE AT PERINEUM

We used 4 Red Jasper with a Smokey Quartz center.
Again we kept to the Cube or square or Hexahedron
The Smokey Quartz in the center serves as a balance.
The Red Jasper is used for energizing.

Our Root Chakra resonates to the color red, contains our basic survival instincts and security issues. Our roots, family, friends, the material word, all of these are housed here. Here is where we carry the power to succeed. The body: everything solid: spine, bones, teeth, nails, legs, arms, intestines, prostate gland, anus, and blood and cell multiplication. It also governs the adrenal glands.

We used Red Jasper for our grid. Here are the properties for that stone:

Red Jasper—supreme nurturer, supportive stone, especially during stressful times, detoxifies liver and dissolves blockages in liver, detoxifies circulatory system and blood. Balancing stone for yin and yang; energizing, stimulating, grounding, a protective stone. Balances mineral content of the body. Place on solar plexus, sacral or base chakras. Aligns all. South Africa

Imbalances in the base or root Chakra could lead to sexual disturbances and feelings of anger, impotence and frustration.

4. SACRAL CHAKRA ABOVE THE PUBIC BONE

We used Orange Carnelian in a 6 stone grid with a Smokey Quartz Center The Tetrahedron. The Orange Carnelian is used to encourage creativity.

Carnelian– Encourages sociability, emotional warmth, individuality, happiness and self-esteem, creativity, memory, appreciation of nature, harmony, courage, acceptance of death and rebirth, past life recall. Carnelian stimulates the absorption of vitamins, nutrients and minerals in the small intestine, thereby improving the quality of the blood ensuring a good supply to the organs and tissues. It alleviates rheumatism, stimulates metabolism. It is best worn in contact with the skin.

Imbalances in this chakra can lead to low self-worth and
low self-esteem

5. THE SOLAR PLEXUS CHAKRA - AT THE WAIST OR JUST BELOW

We used Yellow Jasper 8 stones total in the Ascension Grid or the Tetrahedron. The Yellow Jasper is used for nurturing.

Yellow Jasper— protective stone prevents absorption of negative energies either from environment or other people. Balances yin and yang. Works with liver to assist detoxification of circulatory system and blood. Dissolves blockages in liver and bile ducts. Cleanses aura and aligns chakras, neutralizes environmental radiation. Placed under pillow it helps recall significant dreams. Place directly on skin, it works slowly but effectively. Here is our Universal Connection. In Qigong, the excess energy is stored here for future use.

An imbalance in this Chakra can lead to deep feelings of inferiority.

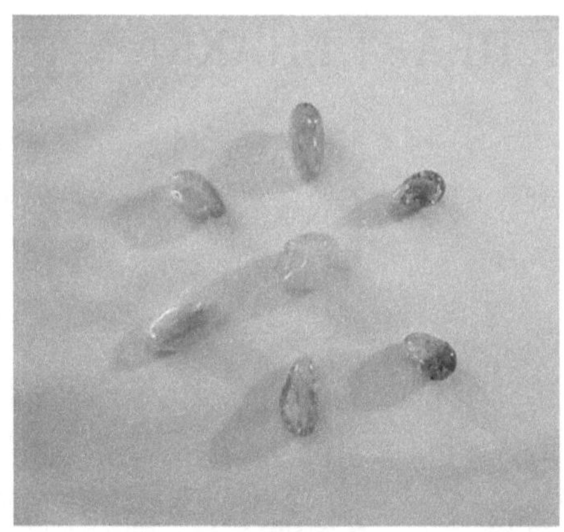

Another grid for the Solar Plexus using 7 Citrine stones in a Tetrahedron

Citrine –Fosters prosperity, creativity, generosity, pleasure, protection, strength. Aligns Yin and Yang, bestows confidence, stability, healing, moderation, comfort, career success, truth and warmth. Citrine stimulates the digestion, promotes the working of the stomach, spleen and pancreas and will alleviate diabetes in its early stages. Should be worn in contact with the skin or placed in areas of the home or business to promote prosperity and abundance, far left hand corner of house or room.

6. THE HEART CHAKRA

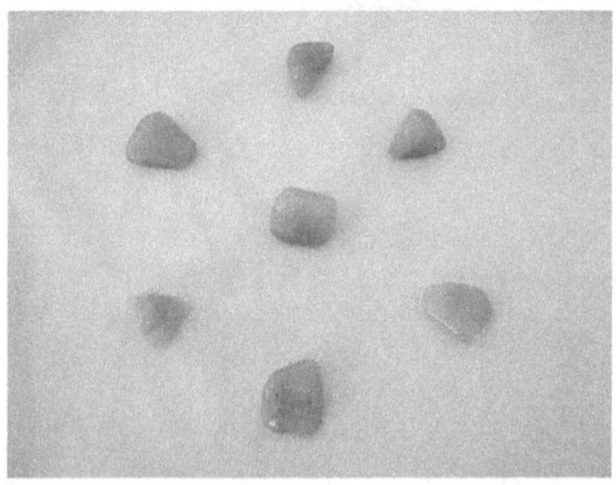

Heart Chakra Grid – We used 7 Green Aventurine to heal emotional distress. .

Green Aventurine—Protects and resonates w/heart chakra for healing. Neutralizes environmental pollution from computers and cell phones. Positive stone for prosperity and attracting abundance. Stabilizes blood pressure, stimulates metabolism, can prevent arteriosclerosis and heart attacks by lowering cholesterol and regenerating heart. Anti-inflammatory, helps with allergies, sooths nausea. Place over spleen to prevent leaching of energy.

Imbalances in the heart chakra can lead to possessiveness and jealousy.

6A SPLEEN CHAKRA – BELOW LEFT ARMPIT

12 Aquamarine with a Clear Crystal center.

Aquamarine—associated with cleansing, meditation, prophecy, serenity, inspiration, tranquility, peace, strength and the wise use of inner power. Calms fears, helps us get in touch with the nature spirits of the sea. Promotes safe travel on water. Harmonizes pituitary and thyroid gland, regulating growth and hormone balance. Improves sight and calms over-reaction of immune system, autoimmune diseases and allergies.

Imbalances in this Chakra are anger issues, and constant irritation. If too open, people can draw on your energy leaving you depleted. Wearing a stone on the left side of the body under the arm can alleviate this.

7. THE HIGH HEART (OR ETHERIC HEART)

This grid is entirely created using 9 Rose Quartz for Unconditional Love.

Rose Quartz- Pink– enhances all forms of love, platonic and romantic love, mother love, self-love, divine love. Encourages tolerance and forgiveness. Opens our hearts and teaches us to be tender, peaceful and gentle. Emanates unconditional love and helps us attract love. Purifies and opens the heart at all levels, strengthens the physical heart and circulatory system. Wear or place over heart or thymus. In Feng Shui, place in relationship corner of room or by your bed. (Far right hand corner)

Imbalances in this Chakra are emotional neediness and

the inability to express feelings openly.

Another Grid for this Chakra:

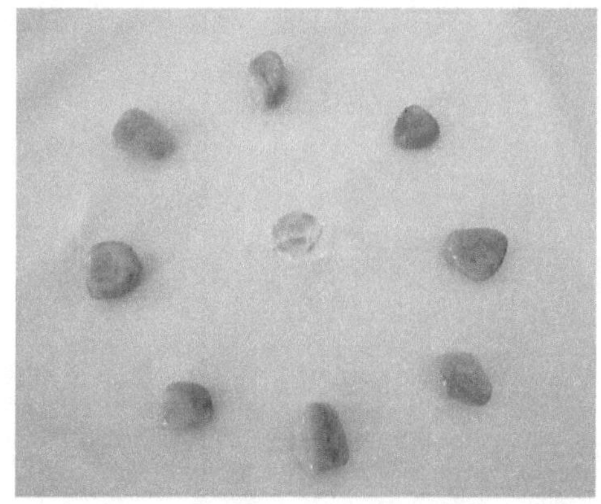

Because this Chakra is placed at the Thymus and is located directly between the heart (green) and the throat (blue) blending these two colors together gives us aqua or turquoise.

Here we used eight Amazonite with a clear crystal Dodecahedron center.

Amazonite - Brazil - Powerful filter - blocks geopathic stress from computers, microwaves and cell phones. Heals the Etheric Heart, opens the Third Eye and Intuition. Dissipates negative energy, blockages in nervous system. Beneficial for osteoporosis, tooth decay, calcium deficiency, deposits.

8. THE THROAT CHAKRA (CENTER OF YOUR THROAT)

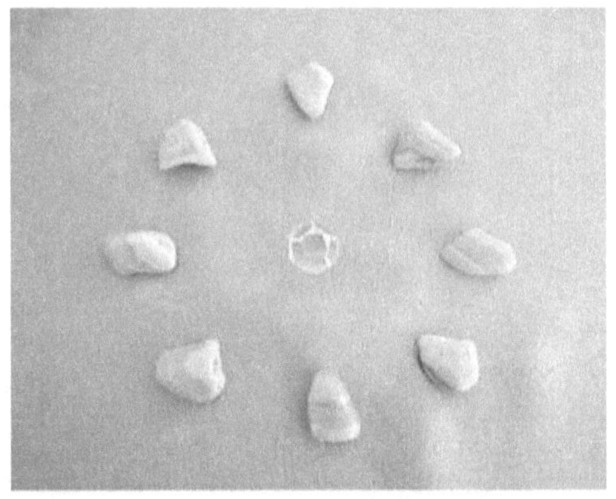

We used 8 Blue Lace Agate with a Clear Crystal Dodecahedron to open communication.

Blue Lace Agate— A nurturing stone, powerful throat healer. Resonates with the throat chakra and is beneficial to conditions of the throat, neck and shoulders. Benefits thyroid and parathyroid. Also resonates with skeletal system, can assist healing of bone fractures and arthritis. Gently removes any feeling of suffocation in the chest, and the physical conditions that arise out of this such as asthma or emphysema. Neutralizes the heat found in fever, infection and anger by gently dissipating any buildup of energy.

An Imbalance in this Chakra leads to a lack of communication where thoughts and feelings cannot be verbalized.

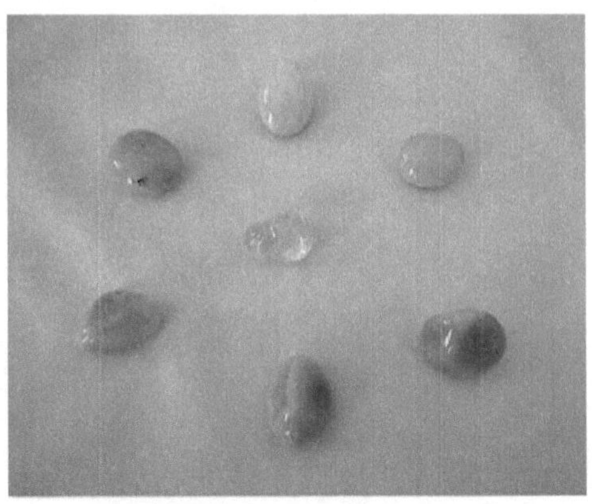

6 Blue Chalcedony with a Citrine crystal for opening communication

Blue Chalcedony-Promotes communication and listening skills, accept new situations, light-heartedness, carefree, optimism, self-awareness, improves perception, memory, calms and dissolves stress. The crystal of orators and diplomats, it facilitates learning foreign languages. Relieves respiratory ailments, lowers blood pressure, edema, enhances immune system, stimulates insulin. Wear on chain or pendant or lay directly on diseased part of body.

9. THE BROW CHAKRA (THIRD EYE – BETWEEN THE EYEBROWS)

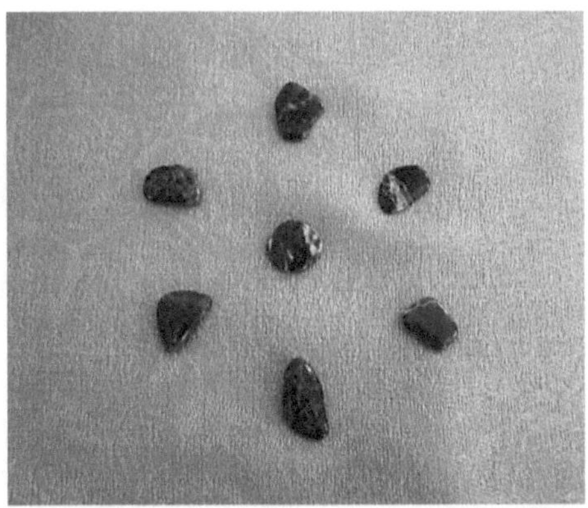

These 7 little Sodalite Chips just wanted to form this grid for Attuning. This grid was humming!

Sodalite-Unites logic w/intuition, clears electromagnetic pollution, brings harmony to group work, and encourages rational thought, objectivity, truth, intuitive perception. Calms panic attacks, emotional balance, enhances self-esteem and self-acceptance. Balances the metabolism, calcium deficiencies, cleanses lymphatic system and organs. Combats radiation damage and insomnia. Cools fevers and lowers blood pressure. Place as appropriate or wear for long periods of time.

Imbalances here can lead to delusion or be overwhelmed by other people's thoughts.

10. CROWN CHAKRA (TOP OF HEAD)

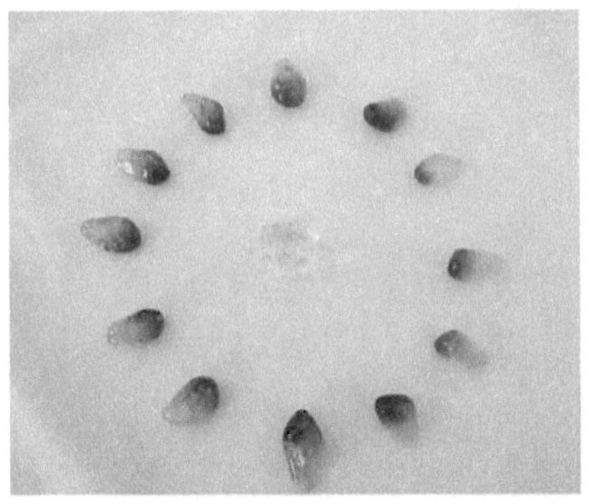

This grid is 12 Amethyst points (Flower of Life) with a center of a Icosederon.in clear crystal for opening intuition.

Amethyst-Quartz. Ranges in color from violet to dark purple. Enhances spiritual awareness, meditation, balance, psychic abilities, inner peace, healing, positive transformation, relieves stress. Brings understanding of death and rebirth. Unlocks spiritual, mystic, psychic wisdom. Is very healing. Worn to prevent drunkenness, overcomes addictions of all kinds. A natural tranquilizer.

Imbalances here can lead to control issues, arrogance.

If stuck open it may lead to obsession or possession.

11. HIGHER CROWN CHAKRA (FORTH DIMENSION)

We used 6 Labradorite and 6 Clear Quartz to create this Flower of Life Grid with a Clear Quartz Icosahedron center to open spiritual communication.

Labradorite - Highly mystical and protective, a bringer of Light, it raises consciousness and connects with universal energies. Deflects unwanted energies from the aura, prevents energy leakage. Aligns the physical and etheric bodies, accesses spiritual purpose. Treats disorders of the eyes and brain, colds, gout, rheumatism. Balances hormones and lowers blood pressure. A stone of transformation, prepares the body and soul for ascension process. Imbalances here can create spiritual untrustworthy, possible entity attachment.

12. HIGHER CROWN CHAKRA (2) FIFTH DIMENSION

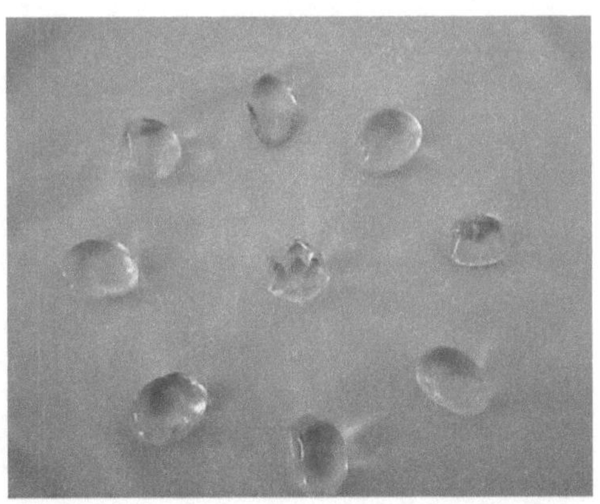

8 Clear Quartz Crystals with a Clear Quartz Icosahedron in the center for reaching enlightenment.

Clear Quartz - The most powerful healing and energy amplifier on the planet. It absorbs, stores, releases and regulates energy and is excellent for unblocking it. Works at a vibrational level attuned to the specific energy requirements of the person holding it. Master healer, it can be used for any condition, stimulates immune systems and brings the body back into balance.

When Spiritual Enlightenment is attained, one is attuned to higher things, enlightened in speech and deeds with true humility.

PAST LIFE CHAKRAS (THREE FINGERS BEHIND YOUR EAR)

A 6 pointed grid with Green Aventurine with a Rose Quartz center stone. This grid is for Past Life Regression.

A 7 stone grid of Orange Carnelian for Past Life Recall.

THE 22ND CHAKRA (SIXTH DIMENSION)

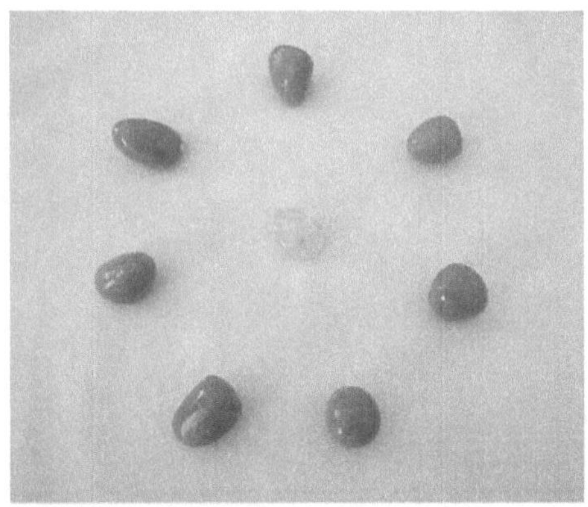

7 Angelite Stones with a center of Citrine.

Angelite- Represents peace and brotherhood, facilitates contact w/Angelic Realm and out-of-body journeys. A Stone for healers. Unblocks meridians when applied to feet. At throat it alleviates inflammation and balances thyroid, and parathyroid. Repairs tissue, blood vessels, balancing body fluids, can act as diuretic. Useful in weight control. Relates to the lungs and arms. Balances physical body with etheric realms.

This is the last Chakra in the fifth dimensional Chakra Grid, the highest level for enlightenment for this dimension.

THE 33RD CHAKRA (EIGHTH DIMENSION)

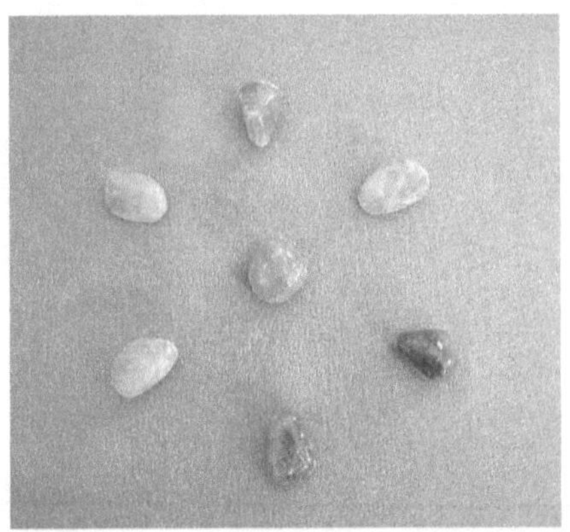

We chose 7 Celestite for this grid with its higher energies.

Celestite - Madagascar - A stone of high vibrations, teacher for New Realms, it is imbued with Divine Energy. Stimulates clairvoyant communications, dream recall and out-of-body journeys. Heals the aura, brings balance and alignment, heals disorders of the eyes and ears, eliminates toxins, and brings cellular order. A large piece placed in a room heightens the vibration. Direct sunlight will fade colors.

This Chakra is in the Eighth Dimensional Hierarchy and signifies the full realization of the Christos or the Christ Consciousness from the Greek.

THE 44ᵀᴴ CHAKRA (TENTH DIMENSION)

Russian Lemurian Ice quartz Crystals. These Ice quartz Stones love linear grids and do not do well in a circular one. Judy Hall wrote about them and from her notes I created a book: *Stones and Bones* which speaks about the healing qualities of these stones.

Russian Lemurian Ice Quartz— Cold, rational and intelligent 'mental' energy. They are excellent for people who are overly emotional and out of control. They have a clarity that there is no getting away from, it's impossible to hide truth in their presence. These stones take you to the 44th chakra which is more a plane of existence. On the soma chakra they reseed ancient knowledge. Wherever placed on the body, energy streams through when activated by sound or touch. They act as a regulating valve connecting opposite and complementary processes. There is an energy release without needing to know what/why. These crystals enable you to see what's at the other end of the wormhole. Origin of these stones: Russia

** There are probably many more dimensions, but for the purposes of this book, we will work with ten.

Also by S. D. Anderson

AVAILABLE IN PRINT ** starred title

Visionary Fiction

Atlantis – The Final Days**

Angels in Action

What Should You Do with Your Life?

Stones and Bones**

Something Sinister**

Visionary Non-Fiction

Creating Crystal Grids**

Sacred Grids**

Crystal Grids for Light Bodies

What Are You Thinking? **

Cosmic Blueprint**

Outer Realms

Raising Your Energy**

Body Blogs for Health**

<u>Children's Book</u>

Tuk-Tuk the Rabbit**

<u>Spiritual Guidelines Series</u>

Prosperity Workbook

Remarkable Relationships

To Your Health**

Everyone is Evolving

<u>ON WRITING</u>

Writing as a Retail Business**

Creating a Paperback in KDP**

E-Book to Paperback CreateSpace Edition**

NOW AVAILABLE IN PRINT ARE STARRED**

ABOUT THE AUTHOR

Sharon D. Anderson, PhD, RMT

S.D. Anderson is an Indie Author/Publisher, dedicated to her craft for more than 30 years. Writing in her genre, Visionary Fiction and Non-Fiction, all of her books, websites and blogs merge a far-seeing perspective of New Age and Ancient Wisdom from Eastern, Western, and Primordial Philosophies.

Living on her beloved Cape Cod, she founded the Cape Cod Writers Studio which meets weekly in Dennis Port.

Here is the link to her Amazon Authors Page:

https://www.amazon.com/author/andersonsharon

E-mail: sdanderson.books@gmail.com